Christmas Through the Eyes of…

A Look at Christmas from the Perspective of
Those Who First Saw It

Christmas Through the Eyes of…

A Look at Christmas from the Perspective of Those Who First Saw It

Kevin Payne

Atlantic Pencraft Publishing

Alexander City, Alabama

Christmas Through the Eyes of...

A Look at Christmas From the Perspective of Those Who First Saw It

Published by Atlantic Pencraft Publishing
Alexander City, Alabama

Copyright 2012 by Kevin Payne

Cover photo of a nativity on the altar of the Dadeville First United Methodist Church in Dadeville, Alabama. Photo courtesy of Bill Brown and the DFUMC Trustees. Used with permission. All rights reserved.

The scripture quotations contained herein are from the New Revised Standard Version Bible, copyright 1989, Division of Christian Education of the National Council of Churches of Christ in the U.S.A. Used by permission. All rights reserved.

Library of Congress Control Number: 2012916973

ISBN-13: 978-1479270149
ISBN 10: 1479270148

Dedication

This work is dedicated to the congregation of the Dadeville First United Methodist Church. Thank you for allowing the breadth of my mission and ministry, and for your loving support. You are an extraordinary people with whom it is a joy to serve.

It is also dedicated, no less, to my wife Melissa. Thank you for taking this journey with me. Together may we grow in grace and love.

Special Thanks

I want to give a special word of thanks to Mr. William Brown, Dr. Adelaide Brown, and Rev. David Carboni. Thank you for exploring this idea with me, editing my drafts, and accompanying me on this journey. Your friendship and mentoring is more precious to me than you can possibly know.

Contents

Prologue

This book began as a sermon series I have preached in my congregation. As I studied the Christmas narratives found in the scriptures, I pondered how those who experienced and lived the first Christmas might have "seen" it. This led me to envision what that first Christmas might have looked like through the eyes of John the Baptizer, Mary, Joseph, the Shepherds, God, and the Magi.

This was a spiritual journey for me, as it challenged many of the ways I thought about and celebrated Christmas. I hope this will be a spiritual journey for you as well. Please remember that the chapters contain my pondering and envisioning of what Christmas *might* have looked like through the eyes of these persons. It is not intended to try to state unequivocally *what* these persons thought about or experienced.

I believe, however, that by carefully considering the passages of scripture that proclaim the story of Christmas we can, in fact, gain some insight as to how this first Christmas might have been experienced by those who dared to live it. As a result of wrestling with these perspectives, our own might be challenged and changed. We just might learn some new aspects of what Christmas means for the world and us. Perhaps we might even be reminded of truths we have forgotten. All I can say is, "Welcome to the journey!"

Introduction

As the song goes, "It's the most wonderful time of the year!"[1] And to be sure, it is! It is a special time when emphasis is given to family and friends, peace, love, and goodwill to all. There is something electrifying about it all. Decorations are everywhere, carols fill the air, and the pure excitement of children help to make the feelings of this time of year unique.

But this can also be a difficult season. For many, this is *not* the "most wonderful time of the year..." From those who do not have family with which to share, or those for whom this is the first Christmas season after the loss of a loved one, those out of work and unable to make ends meet—the list of reasons why this may not be the happiest time goes on and on.

And we need to be honest with ourselves. With all the hustle and bustle of the season, there are not many of us who don't at some point feel as though we are on "Christmas overload!" There is the shopping for just the right gift. There are the struggles of fighting the crowds at the stores. There is the planning and preparing for family gatherings, church cantatas, children's programs, parades, dealing with the in-laws, and the like. I have had more than one person tell me "I'll be so glad when Christmas is over!" It always breaks my heart to hear those words.

We, as Christ's followers, know the true meaning of Christmas. We know the account of his birth. We have heard how Mary and Joseph traveled, how the angels sang, and how the shepherds marveled. We know of mangers, swaddling clothes, and hay. But do we know the true story? Do we know what the account of Christmas as recorded in the gospels seeks to teach, or do we simply know the parts of the story? If we do know what Christmas proclaims, are we living out its message?

Somehow, in the way we live out the Advent and Christmas seasons, we have forgotten what we proclaim Christmas to truly be. We accuse the world of taking Christmas away from us by making it commercialized, and seeking to separate the religious celebration from the celebration of the holiday. But stop and consider this with me for a moment: In reality it is hard to perceive a difference in the way we as Christians keep the holiday and the way the "pagans" do. Are not we just as guilty of commercializing Christmas and forgetting its real meaning as anyone at whom we want to point a finger?

We have forgotten the real story. Perhaps we have never considered what the Christmas narratives found in scripture truly say. Maybe our attention is drawn so much to the images of shepherds, angels, and songs, that we fail to hear their message and testimony. We have made Christmas cute and placid; something that fits well on a Christmas card. We have made Christmas something that is socially acceptable. In fact, we, the Believers, have made it so acceptable that society at large wants it for its own without the burden of it being about the coming of the Christ.

It was scandalous when Jesus was born. There was an unmarried woman pregnant, and claiming to carry the Son of God. She and her betrothed were claiming to have seen visions of angels. There are shepherds straight from the field who come barging in on the newborn child and his family. And don't forget the political unrest going on in the world. Rome had just ordered its first census so that they could institute a new tax.

This is from whence my questions arose. So what was Christmas like for those who first experienced it and dared to proclaim it? That is what this Advent/Christmas reflection is about. We are seeking to catch a glimpse of the message of Christmas without being distracted, or completely blinded, by the tinsel and trimmings.

What did Christmas look like through the eyes of those who lived it when it began? How does John the Baptizer fit within the Christmas narrative? What made Mary special? What did Joseph think when he first heard the news? What is so great about shepherds? What is Christmas to God? Why would Magi from other countries come to worship a Jewish child as a king? These, and questions like them, filled my mind. Yet as I continued to journey, I began to understand something greater about Christmas than I had ever considered before. Perhaps it was obvious. I have to admit I had heard, "God loves you," before. But considering Christmas from these perspectives helped me begin to grasp the depth of that love.

Perhaps by taking this journey together we will wrestle with some of these questions and dare to reclaim the meaning of Christmas in our own lives. Maybe you know the Christmas narratives by heart, or perhaps this is the first time you have ever heard the stories that surround the birth of Jesus. Maybe you fully understand the love God has for you, or perhaps you are unsure whether God can love you. No matter where you are on your journey of faith, it is my prayer for you that after this journey you will never sing "Joy to the World," or for that matter, "It's the Most Wonderful Time of the Year," the same way again.

Can you believe this guy?
What might Christmas look like through the eyes of
John the Baptizer?

The Gospel of John 1:19-29

This is the testimony given by John when the Jews sent priests and Levites from Jerusalem to ask him, "Who are you?" He confessed and did not deny it, but confessed, "I am not the Messiah." And they asked him, "What then? Are you Elijah?" He said, "I am not." "Are you a prophet?" He answered, "no." Then they said to him, "Who are you? Let us have an answer for those who sent us. What do you say about yourself?" He said,
"I am the voice of one crying out in the wilderness,
'Make straight the way of the Lord,'"
As the prophet Isaiah said. Now they had been sent from the Pharisees. They asked him, "Why then are you baptizing if you are neither the Messiah, nor Elijah, nor the prophet?" John answered them, "I baptize with water. Among you stands one whom you do not know, the one who is coming after me; I am not worthy to untie the thong of his sandal." This took place in Bethany across the Jordan where John was baptizing. The next day he saw Jesus coming toward him and declared, "Here is the Lamb of God who takes away the sin of the world!"[2]

Chapter 1

Christmas Through the Eyes of John the Baptizer

AT FIRST LOOK this passage might seem bit odd with which to begin a study about Christmas. After all, shouldn't we be discussing angels and shepherds and such? Here we are talking about John the Baptizer doing what John the Baptizer does— baptizing! John is a grown man, and Jesus is grown and beginning his ministry. Christmas is about the birth, right?

Well, Christmas is about more than a birth. Christmas is the celebration of the Incarnation—the coming of God as one of us. Think about this profound statement: *God became fully human to be with us.* But why? Simply stated, because God loves us. That is some powerful love! Nowhere do the scriptures say it more succinctly than in a passage

11

many of us learned as children. *For God so loved the world that he gave his only Son, so that everyone who believes in him may not perish, but have eternal life. Indeed, God did not send the Son into the world to condemn the world, but in order that the world might be saved through him.*[3]

Christmas is about the coming of the Christ.

In many Christian traditions there is a celebration of a liturgical season called "Advent." The season of Advent begins four Sundays before Christmas. The emphasis of Advent is on preparation. The term "Advent" comes from the Latin "adventus" which literally means "coming." During Advent preparations are made for the coming of the Christ. But these preparations are two-fold. The first is a spiritual preparation to receive anew the gift of the Christ as the Child of the Manger. The second is to remember the promise and prepare for the return of Christ at the Second Coming. To truly celebrate Christmas we must truly prepare!

But we already know that we must prepare for Christmas. Christmas is a big deal! There is so-much-to do, so many places to go, and so many tasks to accomplish. We have a deadline—December 25. It cannot be pushed back simply because we didn't get ready. I mean, as a father, I cannot look at my children on Christmas morning and say, "You know kids, daddy has been really busy the past few weeks. I'm not quite finished with everything I needed to do to prepare for Christmas. So I'll tell you what; we will celebrate Christmas a week from Thursday." No, of course not! We can't postpone Christmas just because we are not ready for it. Christmas is coming. The date is set. We know we must get prepared.

We must recognize that this is exactly what the rest of those in our society who celebrate Christmas think about this season as well. So often when we think of preparing for Christmas our minds turn to decorating, cooking, cleaning, shopping, rehearsing musicals, and the like. Television stations promote special Christmas programming with movies and shows. Some radio stations forgo their regular playlists and program Christmas music all season long. While there is nothing "wrong" with all of this, we must admit that these festive aspects of Christmas more often than not become our focus.

We become so sidetracked with the trimmings and trappings that we forget what Christmas is truly about. It's like getting so involved with wrapping the gift that we forget to put the gift itself inside the box. Then, when the gift is received and opened, all that is found is an empty box!

I have had many people confess to me that Christmas really doesn't feel like Christmas to them anymore. Believe me, I can relate. There was a time when I earnestly wanted to have the feelings of Christmas that I had felt before. I wanted to experience Christmas as I had previously. However, for some reason, those feelings and experiences escaped me. What I found was that I was wrapping the notion of Christmas up like a bright, beautiful gift, but I was leaving the true gift, the true meaning of Christmas, out of my life and my celebrations.

It really cannot feel like *Christ*mas if *Christ* is not in it. I found that this blessed season calls us to slow down and consider what is happening. It is true, we must prepare for Christmas. And make no mistake; I do not believe that the social and personal traditions that surround its celebration are wrong. It is simply that they need to be kept in proper perspective. We must come to the realization that it is our choice as to how we prepare for Christmas. How we prepare for it will determine how we feel about it and experience it. If we want to encounter Christmas as a meaningful, powerful, vital celebration of grace and love, then it is imperative for us to prepare in ways that are truly spiritually significant.

That is why we begin with asking the question, "What might Christmas look like through the eyes of John the Baptizer?" What John the Baptizer is proclaiming is to prepare! John is not advocating for us to be sure that we get the Christmas tree up in time, or the Christmas cards in the mail, or to have the menu for Christmas dinner planned. Of course, we know that already! So what is John's call for preparation about? To put it simply, John the Baptizer's proclamation calls us to prepare our hearts and lives for the coming of the Christ.

In considering John's message, it might help to

contemplate about John the Baptizer personally. We know a little about him. The gospel according to Luke records his annunciation and birth. [4]

His father, Zechariah, served as a priest. While Zechariah was serving at the Temple, specifically offering incense in the Sanctuary, the angel Gabriel appeared to him. Gabriel told him that his wife, Elizabeth, would conceive in her old age. He would name the child John, and John *will turn many of the people of Israel to the Lord their God. With the spirit and power of Elijah he will go before him* [the Messiah], *to turn the hearts of parents to their children, and the disobedient to the wisdom of the righteous, to make ready a people prepared for the Lord.*[5] In fact, when Mary goes to visit Elizabeth, John leaps in his mother's womb.[6] We know John the Baptizer is going to have a special calling and ministry. He is the one who is sent to prepare the way of the Lord![7]

John does grow and live into his special calling and ministry. We see this exemplified in several of the gospels. However, John also would have been a bit scandalous. He is, after all, in the wilderness crying out about repentance. He wears camel's hair clothing, a leather belt, and eats locusts and wild honey.[8] Now imagine the folks that stand on the streets in New York City with their signs and megaphones proclaiming something about God, or the world coming to an end. How do we tend to perceive them? Yet here is John, the one we call the Baptizer, engaging in a similar exercise. What might be shocking to us is the fact that people are responding![9] John is living out his ministry to prepare the way of the Lord.

That is what we read in the opening scripture passage. John is going about his calling and ministry. He is proclaiming the coming of the Lord. He is calling for people to prepare their hearts for that which God is seeking to do in their lives.

In this passage we hear John's proclamation. As John looks up and sees Jesus coming, the day after he [John] had been questioned by the religious authorities, he declares, *Here is the Lamb of God who takes away the sin of the world!*[10] This moment, this proclamation, becomes in many ways the climax of John's ministry.

If we continue reading in John 1:30 and following we would see that again, on the next day, John sees Jesus coming and makes the same proclamation. Two of John's disciples leave him and follow after Jesus. We see John the Baptizer accomplishing what he was sent to do. John the Baptizer is preparing.

This is our response to the declaration of John the Baptizer. In fact, this is how we truly prepare for Christmas. Preparing is not about outward appearance and social engagements. The outward is not what is most important. Consider what Jesus said to the scribes and Pharisees in Matthew 23:25-28

Woe to you, scribes and Pharisees, hypocrites! For you clean the outside of the cup and the plate, but inside they are full of greed and self-indulgence. You blind Pharisee! First clean the inside of the cup, so that the outside also may become clean.

Woe to you, scribes and Pharisees, hypocrites! For you are like whitewashed tombs, which on the outside look beautiful, but inside they are full of the bones of the dead and of all kinds of filth.

So you also on the outside look righteous to others, but inside you are full of hypocrisy and lawlessness.[11]

These are some very abrasive words! However, they are words with which we truly need to wrestle. Jesus is speaking truth we need to hear.

How, in the ways we typically prepare for Christmas, do we simply "wash the outside of the cup"[12] or "whitewash a tomb"[13] and claim that we are celebrating the gift of the Christ in our lives? Do we truly expect to receive the Incarnation? Do we really look for the second coming of the Christ? How is this seen and lived out in the ways we observe the Advent of our Lord; in the ways we celebrate Christmas?

The response to the call that John the Baptizer is daring to proclaim is to do as two of his disciples did. These two chose to leave John and follow Jesus, thereby becoming Jesus' first two disciples. These two disciples dared to leave all they thought they knew in order to follow where the Christ was going.

That is what John's call for preparation to us is about, as well. Are we prepared to leave what we think we know and dare to truly follow? If it is not for this—if it is not for a life being lived following our Lord and Savior—then what are we preparing for?

We are not only called to *prepare* to follow Jesus, but are called to *actually* follow. This is an invitation that requires action, not simply planning. The preparation for which John the Baptizer is advocating cannot be accomplished by sitting on the sideline with a notebook sketching all of the details of what we perceive we must accomplish in order to "prepare." There is no course of study that replaces the admonition to arise and follow. There are no intellectual exercises whereby we can understand and assemble all of the pieces, and then begin the task.

The Christ has come to be the Lamb of God who takes away the sin of the world.[14] There is strategic movement in this proclamation. Christ is active, laboring, on the move, taking away the sin of the world. Now, today, in this moment, Christ is at work in the world. Now, today, in this moment, we are being called to actively follow.

I believe that is what Christmas through the eyes of John the Baptizer would look like. It is preparing through living. It is a life crying out, "Look! Here he is right now! The Lamb of God is here today to take away the sins of the world!"[15] It is urgent. It is immediate. It is occurring now!

As we have already mentioned, we know about socially preparing for Christmas. But now we are wrestling with the notion that those preparations are not what make Christmas, well, Christmas. They are not central to the true celebration of the Christmas season. The preparations of food, gifts, and the like are not the preparations for which John is calling us. The physical preparations for the traditions of family and such are important to us. And, again, make no mistake, when kept in their proper perspective, they are not wrong. But we must realize these do not make the importance of Christmas. As Dr. Seuss's Grinch learned, Christmas comes even if there are no ribbons, tags, packages, boxes, or bags![16]

So often the shopping, and the cooking, and the decorating, and the traveling, and so forth crowd out what we claim to be most important. If we believe that society at large should, "keep Christ in Christmas," should not we, as those professing to be Christ's followers, be demonstrating by our actions how? But let us be honest with ourselves and ask a tough, personal question: Does our hustle and bustle look any different than the rest of society at large? Do we, in our own lives, really keep Christ in Christmas?

Christmas through the eyes of John the Baptizer is about a time of preparing our hearts and lives for the coming of the Christ. This is a time to prepare to welcome the Child of the Manger. It is a call to prepare for the return of the King of Kings. It is a season about hope, peace, love and joy. It is not about angels, shepherds, and mangers simply as pieces of a proper holiday display. It is about the angel's song, the shepherd's message, and the manger's contents. The Christmas proclamation is "good news of great joy to all people."[17] It is about the Savior of the World who is born in Bethlehem as one of us. It is about beholding the Lamb of God who has come to take away our sin, and the sins of the entire world!

So, what are we going to do with John's message? What are we going to do with how Christmas can be perceived through his eyes? Are we going to continue through this special time of year as we have in the past? Are we going to sing along with the carols with our mouths while our hearts are far away? Are we going to take on all of the perceived requirements to make a "perfect holiday," accepting the stress that accompanies such, while inwardly desiring it to hurry and end? In short, are we going to miss the genuine celebration of Christmas, or are we going to prepare?

Are we going to prepare not only our homes and schedules, but our hearts and lives as well? I hope so! I pray we are too excited, too nervous, too anxious to do anything before we dare to proclaim, as John the Baptizer did, *Here is the Lamb of God who takes away the sin of the world!*[18] I hope we have a desire to share with the entire world the true joy and grace this season proclaims.

May we dare to prepare in the very way we live our lives for the coming of the Christ; to prepare for the first and the second comings. I hope its not simply by bumper stickers, car magnets, t-shirts, and decorative nativity scenes that we tell of the coming of the Messiah. I pray we live differently, so that the world might take notice.

We have a Savior! We have a God who has dared to come and be with us. Prepare! Through the eyes and proclamation of John the Baptizer may we truly behold the Lamb of God.

This is what I imagine Christmas might look like though John's eyes. What does Christmas look like through yours?

Thoughts From Chapter 1

What does it mean that "Christmas is the celebration of the Incarnation—the coming of God as one of us?" How does this impact our lives?

Thinking about this personally, what are ways in which you "forget" what preparing for Christmas is really about?

What are some ways you can keep all of the wonderful traditions that surround the celebration of Christmas while keeping focus on the true meaning?

How can this be?

Contemplating Christmas through the eyes of Mary.

The Gospel of Luke 1:26-38

In the sixth month the angel Gabriel was sent by God to a town in Galilee named Nazareth, to a virgin engaged to a man whose name was Joseph, of the house of David. The virgin's name was Mary. And he came to her and said, "Greetings, favored one! The Lord is with you." But she was much perplexed by his words and pondered what sort of greeting this might be. The angel said to her, "Do not be afraid, Mary, for you have found favor with God. And now you will conceive in your womb and bear a son, and you will name him Jesus. He will be great, and will be called the Son of the Most High, and the Lord God will give to him the throne of his ancestor David. He will reign over the house of Jacob forever, and of his kingdom there will be no end." Mary said to the angel, "How can this be, since I am a virgin?" The angel said to her, "The Holy Spirit will come upon you, and the power of the Most High will overshadow you; therefore the child to be born will be holy; he will be called the Son of God. And now, your relative Elizabeth in her old age has also conceived a son; and this is the sixth month for her who was said to be barren. For nothing will be impossible with God." Then Mary said, "Here am I, the servant of the Lord; let it be with me according to your word." Then the angel departed from her.[19]

25

Chapter 2

Christmas Through the Eyes of Mary

PATRICK JENKINS, WHO was a missionary to South America, told this story:

My family and I had been living in the jungles of South America for a few years and had moved a few times. Facing yet another move, we knew all too well the discomforts of dealing with such things as snakes and bugs. One morning, a few days after beginning to clean out for our new temporary home, we were taking a break. While we were enjoying our tea, a large, black beetle suddenly flew through our tent making a loud, buzzing noise. As it darted between us, my wife let out an even louder scream. Astonished more by her mother's scream than the beetle our youngest daughter cried out, "For heaven's sake Mom!" to which my wife quickly retorted, "That's the only reason why I'm here!"[20]

I believe the same could be said for many of us as well! With the Christmas season being so busy already, taking time for special worship services, devotions, cantatas, and even Bible study can seem to interrupt our plans and schedules. Sometimes it can seem that there is just "one more thing to do" in an already hectic time. However, being interrupted is an important part of Christmas. Really, that is what Christmas itself does. Christmas interrupts us.

Christmas comes roaring in with no real care as to what we already had going. Christmas arrives and declares a breaking of regular routines and systematic approaches to the daily grind. Sure, we know when it is on the calendar, but are we *really* ever expecting it? Christmas seems to call a holy "time-out" of our lives. Christmas invites us to stop what we are doing and consider anew the gift of the Christ. Christmas urges us to see others as our neighbors, and to love them as we love ourselves, as Christ commanded us.[21]

Christmas displays the love of God to us and to the world. Christmas might even bring to light aspects of our lives that we have neglected and cause us to reconsider what is truly important. It is so incredibly easy to be drawn more and more to the work and schedules of our days, even to the exclusion of our spouse or significant other, our children, our parents, our friends; to all the people and things we are so quick to label as "truly important."

As a pastor I have had the difficult privilege of being with many people as they breathed their last breaths and transitioned from this life. Often these times come with confessions of sorts. These conversations tell of regrets and burdens that they have carried with them. Now, at the end, there is nothing they can do to resolve them. Never once have I had any person tell me they wished they had one more day to spend at the office. Not one time has someone confessed to me they would like the chance to climb one more rung on the social ladder. No one has ever expressed to me a desire for one last chance to invest one more dollar in a new lucrative opportunity.

What some have spoken of as regrets always involved lost relationships with family and friends, time not spent with children, never sharing their possessions or their friendship and love with others, and never taking the time to enjoy the life around them. Therein lies the beauty of being interrupted. There is shock and upheaval to our lives. Interruptions are, by their very natures, unexpected. Interruptions barge in without calling ahead to make appointments. We cannot ignore an interruption. And with the interruption comes a new outlook; a new vision.

Christmas, at its heart, at the very beginning, was an interruption. We see this very clearly in the above passage telling about the *Annunciation*—the visit of the angel Gabriel to Mary with the invitation to be the Mother of God. Talk about an interruption! What did Mary think of this? What did she feel? What made Mary so special that God would choose her above all others? This brings us to the question, "What might Christmas look like through the eyes of Mary?" Let us ponder this for a moment. Let's consider what the passage is saying, and imagine what Mary might have been experiencing.

Before this passage we have not heard of Mary. Her name is recorded in the genealogy of Jesus that is found in the first chapter of the gospel of Matthew,[22] but there is no information in the gospels about her origins. Her parents are not mentioned. We do not possess any descriptions of her. Seemingly Mary is just an ordinary young woman, engaged to an ordinary man, in some ordinary village.

Nazareth was a place of importance in the prophecies, but, at the time of Jesus' birth it was not a major metropolis. It does not appear that Mary is some aristocrat's daughter who held some high social standing. Mary seems to be a respectable girl. Perhaps she was well liked. Maybe she was beautiful. Maybe she had a sweet personality, or maybe she was quick-witted and a little feisty. The fact is that no one knows.

There is nothing specific about Mary that tells us why she was chosen by God and called to such a task as bearing the Son into the world. In fact, it seems that Mary is simply going about her ordinary routine, in an ordinary day, at an ordinary place, when the most extraordinary event occurs. An angel interrupts Mary's life!

We can see in other passages of scripture that when people are interrupted by angels God is about to do something world changing. Take a look at Genesis 18 where angelic visitors go to Abraham to tell him and his wife they are going to have a son. Consider Daniel 8 where Gabriel explains an apocalyptic vision that God had given to Daniel about the fall and rise of world powers after intense persecution. Even in Luke 1, where Gabriel visits Zachariah and announces the prelude to the coming of the Messiah, we see God is about to do something big that calls Zachariah and Elizabeth to an extraordinary journey.

When angels "show up," God is about to "show out!" As you read these passages, and even others found in scripture, it seems that angelic announcers never made an appointment. We never see God send a holy email to let people know to be prepared for an angel to visit with them tomorrow. There is never a phone call made to check schedules and see what works the best for everyone. Angels just appear to those for whom God has a message.

Along with the notion of angels just appearing, let's ponder the actual angelic encounter. Have we ever considered the appearing of an angel? We imagine angels as beautiful and glorious. I have always seen angels depicted as radiant, gentle, and strikingly gorgeous. In fact, a term in our vernacular used to denote a peaceful and graceful appearance is "angelic." But is this what we see in the scriptures?

Quite frankly, it seems that those to whom angels appeared were more often than not terrified! This is not too difficult to believe if we think about it for a moment. There you are, going about your daily business, when all of a sudden there is an angel standing before you! Can we imagine looking up and beholding an angel, with wings unfurled bathed in glorious radiance, towering over us delivering some awesome message from God?

And don't forget *what* the angels announce. It is never that God wants to give us a new car, or we have won the lottery, or that we can have our best life now. Angels always seem to announce some grand, world-changing, plan of God. Angels not only announce such a plan, but also are sent to tell individuals that God has called them to *take part in it*! This is a far cry from the images of angels that adorn most nativity scenes. This is not the way I have ever envisioned angels as they are typically portrayed at the yearly children's Christmas pageant.

Looking specifically at the angelic encounter between Mary and Gabriel, not only is it amazing that an angel visits her, but what Gabriel tells Mary is overwhelming. Gabriel's greeting is powerful. The angel's words are inviting, but powerful nonetheless: "Mary, you are chosen by God to be the mother of the Savior of the world."[23] Talk about having your schedule interrupted! If the vision of Gabriel did not inundate Mary, then the opening line surely would have.

This passage stirs such imagery for us. I do not know about you, but I can't help imagining this scene. It has been a favorite theme for artists over the years. For me, whenever I read this, I envision a beautiful, young lady startled off her feet by a heavenly angel dressed in white and glowing with radiance. The scene is tranquil, but majestic. The vision is reserved, yet powerful.

I have heard this account and read this passage more times than I can count. In fact, I can't recall the first time I ever heard it; it seems I grew up knowing it. But I can recall when something it teaches struck me for the very first time. I have always put Mary at the center of the story, with Gabriel in a very close supporting role. But that is not the case. Mary is not the central figure in this passage, nor is Gabriel. The central figure in this story is God.

Why, even though we know the Bible to be fundamentally about God, do we fail to see this event, the Annunciation, as being primarily about God? I believe it is because as long as we do not perceive it as being about God, then we can be removed from it and from its call.

Consider this. As long as we see it being about Mary, then there must be *something* about her that makes her more special than us. Even though it may not be mentioned in scripture, for her to be chosen for such a world changing, daunting calling there must be something that makes her not so ordinary as us. As long as the focus is on Mary, we have no part in the story. We become simple observers to the historical account of the birth of the Messiah. We can celebrate it as a marked event in our faith, but not be burdened with the notion that it describes something about our callings as well.

Next there is the angel. As long as we keep Gabriel as a major figure, then we can ignore the possibility of God calling us to some great task. We can say to ourselves, "See, God sends angels to people for whom God wants a big commitment." If you or I have never had a glorious angelic visitor with wings unfurled, something at least one as grand as the encounter described here with Mary, then we must be okay where we are. As long as we see this passage primarily about Gabriel, then we can believe that as long as there are no angels that visit us, then we have no calling to some impossible mission.

Finally there is the message itself. Some have a tendency to see this passage as being primarily about the message that is delivered, rather than about the One who sends it. It is not so difficult to comprehend why we would love this account of the Annunciation to be specifically about a message. A message is dated. A message is specific. The instructions of this message are completed. We can account it to a person, Mary, for the specific task of bearing the Son of God. We can then easily reduce it to a glorious memory, a historic teaching, a truth about God's love to us.

Also, in doing so, we can say that such a mammoth calling was personal to Mary at that time and place. As long as we see this scripture as being about the message itself, then we can pacify ourselves with the belief that God would not call us to some vast undertaking that would require what it did of Mary. Again, we can salve our faith and avoid what God might be calling us to undertake. Therefore, the message spoken cannot be calling us to participate in the mission of Christmas.

However, the moment we come to view this passage as being first and foremost about God, then all that changes. It becomes an account of God's unmerited grace, divine calling, and omnipotent power. It can no longer be reduced to being about the person whom God calls, the manner in which God calls, or the specific message of the call.

When we come to perceive this passage as being primarily about God, then we are forced to wrestle with the notion that there truly is nothing super-special about Mary, of Mary's own accord. What makes her special, what constructs Mary as extraordinary, is her willingness to fully allow her life to be lived in the service of God, for whatever ends God willed.

By accepting the call of God, Mary became remarkable. By yielding her life to God's will, Mary became a heroine of faith. When we see God as the primary figure in this passage, and accept that Mary is ordinary just like us, then we are required to acknowledge that if God can call ordinary Mary to such an extraordinary life of self-sacrifice and service, then God can call ordinary you and ordinary me to the extraordinary as well.

When we start to understand this passage as being about God, then we also have to rethink what it means to be "favored" or "blessed" by God. After all, Gabriel says, "hello" to Mary by saying, "Greetings, favored one!" So we know God favors Mary, and that God is going to bless Mary. But what do these blessings look like compared to what we normally associate as blessings?

Come now, we must admit it. We have a tendency to think of blessings in self-beneficial terms. We ask for God's blessings in ways that we perceive as advantageous. We normally equate having good health as a blessing. We perceive possessions as blessings. How many times have we seen someone driving a nice car with a tag or a bumper sticker reading, "Another Blessing," or "Blessed"? Do we not believe that being able to live in a nice home is a blessing? What about having good food? Do we not give thanks before we eat for the blessing of food, at least when we are at a church potluck?

To be sure, such things are blessings. After all, the scriptures teach us that *every good and perfect gift comes from above.*[24] Godly stewardship of the material that enables nice cars and wonderful homes are blessings. Food is a blessing, after all, who caused it to grow? But what does this naming of only "good" things as blessings imply? How do we interpret "blessing"?

Do we believe that those whom God loves who have health problems are not blessed? Do we believe that those who cannot afford a car are not blessed? Does God reject those who are homeless? What about people in the world that are starving? Does God not care for those who hunger?

Our instinct is to equate blessings with material possessions and physical wellbeing. But let's consider how Mary is going to be blessed by God as one who was favored: She is going to have a child out of wedlock. In her time, in her location, and within her culture, this could have resulted in her being stoned to death. She faces rejection by her community. Her espoused could break the engagement and expose her to public disgrace.

She will have a son, whom she has borne, diapered, run to when he fell, wiped his eyes when he cried, comforted when he was afraid and had a bad dream, and a son whom she witnessed grow into man. That man, her son, Jesus, will be labeled a criminal. Jesus, her son, whom she loves as his mother, will be rejected by her religious leaders, tried as a heretic and traitor, stripped, tortured, beaten, crucified, and killed. Mary will witness all of this, and experience it, not only as a disciple, but *as his mother.* No wonder Simeon told Mary when Jesus was presented at the Temple, *a sword will pierce your own soul too.*[25] Is this what we think of when we ponder being "blessed"?

When we see this passage in this light, and hear the invitation of Gabriel as being sent from God, we recognize that, just as Mary was called and chosen, so too are we. We cannot forget that Jesus' call to those who would follow is, *If any want to become my followers, let them deny themselves and take up their cross daily and follow me. For those who want to save their life will lose it, and those who lose their life for my sake will save it. What does it profit them if they gain the whole world, but lose or forfeit themselves?*[26]

When we see this passage as being all about God and witness it through the eyes of Mary, we see this commandment of the Christ already being lived out. It becomes a powerful example of the calling of God. And we, who profess to follow, cannot escape it.

Acceptability, prosperity, and comfort have never really ever been the essence of God's blessing, no matter how hard we desire it to be. We are all chosen to step out in faith and do the will of God for our lives. We forget that sometimes that which God is calling us to undertake will not be accepted by our society. The life of faith is one that challenges the way things are.

Mary was involved in a social scandal by being unwed and pregnant. However, the ultimate scandal is that God would enter human life. God dared to enter our lives, with all the sin of humanity, with all our sin, and be crucified with it. This is after God dares to live a life as one of us to show us the way.

I believe this is what Christmas through the eyes of Mary would look like. It would demand sacrifice. Mary was willing to answer the call of God into something she did not fully know or understand. She allowed her life to be "interrupted." She was willing to be employed in the will and for the purposes of God.

Mary was an ordinary person, just like us, called to do an extraordinary task, just like us. She has become extraordinary because she had the faith and courage to say "Yes" to God. Now, as is stated in Church tradition, she is the Queen of Heaven. Ordinary becomes extraordinary in the power of God.

Christmas contemplated though the eyes of Mary is about being open and willing to the call of God. It is about self-sacrifice, as Mary's life shows. How is Christmas contemplated through your eyes?

Thoughts From Chapter 2:

How does Christmas "interrupt" us? How does Christmas "interrupt" your life specifically?

How does seeing this passage as being primarily about God challenge our understanding of it? How does this speak to our understanding of what God might call us to undertake?

How does this understanding stretch or challenge our notions of what it means to be "blessed?"

From personal reflection, what are you called to sacrifice in your life? How are you being called to serve? What is hindering or stopping you?

What did you say?

Perceiving Christmas through Joseph's Eyes.

The Gospel of Matthew 1:18-25

Now the birth of Jesus took place in this way. When his mother Mary had been engaged to Joseph, but before they lived together, she was found to be with child from the Holy Spirit. Her husband Joseph, being a righteous man and unwilling to expose her to public disgrace, planned to dismiss her quietly. But just when he had resolved to do this, an angel of the Lord appeared to him in a dream and said, "Joseph, son of David, do not be afraid to take Mary as your wife, for the child conceived in her is from the Holy Spirit. She will bear a son, and you are to name him Jesus, for he will save his people from their sins." All this took place to fulfill what had been spoken by the Lord throughout the prophet:
"Look, the virgin shall conceive and bear a son,
and they shall name him 'Emmanuel,'
which means 'God is with us.'"
When Joseph awoke from sleep, he did as the angel of the Lord commanded him; he took her as his wife, but had no marital relations with her until she had borne a son; and he named him Jesus.[27]

Chapter 3

Christmas Through the Eyes of Joseph

WE DO NOT KNOW much about Joseph. We know his lineage to King David thanks to the first chapter of the *Gospel of Matthew.*[28] However, Joseph is not found in many places throughout the gospel accounts. In fact, Joseph only appears in the Christmas and few childhood narratives about Jesus.

What we know from scripture is he is there for Jesus' birth,[29] the visit of the Magi, and the escape to and return from Egypt.[30]

We see Joseph in the account of Jesus' presentation at the Temple.[31] On another occasion, Joseph was a part of leaving Jesus at the Temple on a trip to celebrate the Passover![32] He and Mary were already on their way home when they noticed Jesus was not with them. It is fearful enough for a parent to lose a child, but can we imagine losing the Son of God!

By the time Jesus begins his ministry as a grown man, however, Joseph is no longer directly in the narrative. Most believe this is because Joseph had died. But even in the scriptural narratives where Joseph is mentioned we aren't told too much about Joseph himself. What we do know is that Joseph is a carpenter, in the family line of King David, and is engaged to Mary.

We understand from the preceding scripture that Joseph knew of Mary being with child before he received his angelic dream. We know this because when the account begins Joseph is pondering what to do. It is not a difficult assumption to make that Mary being found to be with child is a burden for him. We understand he was struggling discerning what to do and how to handle the situation in which he found himself.

But why? Who wouldn't be overjoyed at the notion of the Savior of the World coming? Here and now the long-awaited promise of God is being fulfilled! Joseph is being called to take part in this wonderful gift of the first Christmas. But let's think about this for a minute from Joseph's perspective.

We need to take a moment to understand some of the culture of first-century Palestine, especially with regard to engagement and marriage. So often we consider Joseph and Mary's engagement as being similar to ours. We think of them as dating and

Joseph "popping the question." But in reality, first-century Jewish engagement was not at all like our modern understandings and what we associate with it.

In our modern, western-cultured engagements, those who are engaged are not yet considered married. But in first-century Palestine and specifically in Jewish culture, a woman engaged, or espoused, was considered as one who was married. It was expected that she would be treated with the respect deserving of a married woman, even though they were not "actually" married.

This designation of being engaged or espoused allowed for a new level to the courtship measures. When first "dating," if you will allow the use of the term, Mary and Joseph could not be without an escort. To help us in our understandings grasp this notion, this included walking down the street, going to a store, or sitting on Mary's parent's front porch. No dowry had been paid, and Mary would have still been considered to be a part of her father's family.

But when they became engaged all that changed. Mary has not moved in with Joseph, but she is going to see him. Once engaged, Mary and Joseph could go places together without an escort. More than likely, Mary visited Joseph's shop, cooked him lunch, and talked with him. A dowry had been paid, and Mary was now considered to be a part of Joseph's family. Though not "officially" married, living together, or consummating their relationship, their being a couple was socially and legally recognized. As such, an engagement could only be ended by a divorce.[33] At the time of this scripture, Joseph and Mary are not "married" yet, but they are engaged, with all of the social and legal understanding of what it was to be engaged.

So, how did Joseph learn that Mary had been chosen by God to be the mother of the Christ? This is one possible way: Perhaps one day Mary came to visit Joseph at his shop. It would not have been unusual for her to come by. She would have been by several times before. She would have cooked him something to eat. She would have talked with him about the upcoming wedding. Perhaps she was already telling him how she wanted to rearrange "their" house when the time came for her to move in. It would not have been unusual for Mary to come see Joseph, but something about this day was different.

Perhaps Mary was quieter than usual. Possibly Mary carried an expression on her face that normally would not be found upon her brow. Courtship in this culture took some time. Joseph would have partially understood and been learning Mary and her personality. This is just as we come to know and are learning our spouses and significant others today, with their moods and personalities.

Perchance Joseph saw Mary walk into his carpentry shop. He looked up and said, "Hello!" to her. But this day Mary simply smiled back, rather than giving her usual greeting. Perhaps Joseph stopped his work, walked over to Mary and took her by the hands. Maybe he looked deep into her eyes and asked, "What's up? I know there is something on your mind." Possibly it was then, when Mary looked up into Joseph's eyes, that she began to tell him all that the angel Gabriel had told her. Conceivably it was then that Mary told Joseph that she was with child by the Holy Spirit.

Could Joseph have been anything but surprised, confused, even angry? God had not done anything like this before. It is stated in the scripture that Joseph was a "righteous man."[34] The term "righteous" has certain implications in scripture. As a righteous man, Joseph would have been obedient to the Law, as he would have studied and known the scriptures.[35] He would have gone weekly to the synagogue. He would have made pilgrimage to the Temple in Jerusalem for the special religious celebrations. He surely was brought up in a Jewish home and taught the Jewish faith.

For anyone to come and suggest that God would come as a child born of a woman would have been outrageous. This was not the way Joseph, or any other Jewish person for that matter, was expecting the Messiah to come. This was not the way the prophets and the writings had previously been interpreted.

But for Joseph, this isn't just anyone coming and making such a claim. He had not heard of this outrageous proclamation in passing as he walked down the street. He did not hear this fantastic story in the synagogue parking lot after a Sabbath service. Rather, he hears it from Mary, <u>his</u> betrothed!

Here is Joseph, engaged to a women he deeply loves, who is standing in his shop telling him she is pregnant. Joseph and she both know that he is not the father. This would be impossible to hear anyway, but then she told him how she became with child.

He was not to worry or be upset, for she had not been unfaithful. Mary had not broken the espousal covenant and committed adultry. She was still a virgin. This is because, and here's the good news, the child conceived in her is directly from God! The Holy Spirit came upon her and caused her to become with child. This is not procreation Mary is talking about. Rather, this is *incarnation*! What would you think if <u>your</u> fiancée came to you and told you she was with child from God? I imagine that Joseph either thought something horrible had happened to Mary and she had lost her mind, or Mary was taking him for a fool!

It is obvious that Joseph loves Mary deeply, even more than himself. How do we arrive at this assumption? Because in the passage we have read from Matthew, it appears Joseph has been awake most of the night going over in his mind what Mary had told him. He came to the conclusion to "dismiss her quietly," that is, divorce her without bringing her to the religious leaders of the town, so as to not put upon her public disgrace and endanger her life. But when word got out that the marriage was off, as the word tends to get out in small towns, who would take the blame for instigating the divorce? Joseph would.

We know Joseph was a righteous man, one who was obedient and kept the law. But he could not let Mary be hurt. He loved her and could not bear the thought of her being stoned to death. He would put her away quietly, absent from the community's eye. Then, when it became public knowledge that the wedding was off, he would accept responsibility for it.

When Joseph had determined what he thought he was going to do, he fell asleep. I do not believe this was peaceful slumber that arrives when a problem is resolved, but rather sheer exhaustion and depression that took its toll. Of course, as Woody Allen is credited with saying, "If you want to make God laugh, tell him your plans."[36] Though I do not believe God was laughing at what Joseph had resolved to do or at the struggles Joseph was facing, I do know God had a different idea.

I believe God was not only calling Mary to an extraordinary journey, but Joseph as well. As Joseph slept God sent an angelic messenger to him, just as God had sent to Mary. In the encounter, the angel tells Joseph that Mary is, in fact, with child of the Holy Spirit. She has not been unfaithful, and Joseph should not be afraid to take her as his wife.

In this dream Joseph learns that the promise of the Messiah is being fulfilled in a way no one expected. The Christ is coming as one of us, in order to put a right heart within us,[37] and restore us to a right relationship with God. The Messiah was coming for the entire world in order to save the world from sin and its ravages. A verse from the prophet Isaiah foretold that the Messiah would come in this way: *Look, the virgin shall conceive and bear a son, and they shall name him Emmanuel.*[38] I wonder if Joseph remembered ever reading that passage after the angel quoted it?

Here we learn a new aspect about the righteousness of God. Righteousness is not only keeping the laws and commandments, but it is sacrificial love, too. We cannot overlook that it is Mary *and* Joseph who are called to be the parents of the Christ. I believe God knew the depths of Joseph's love for Mary. I know God knew of Joseph's genuine love for God. Perhaps Joseph's deep, sacrificial love for God and for Mary is what made him the perfect earthly father for God's own Son.

I cannot begin to imagine what was racing through Joseph's mind when he awoke from this dream. Was he afraid? Now he knew he was going to be the earthly father of God's Son. Was he overjoyed that he found out Mary was true to him? Was he humbled that God had chosen *them* to be the parents of the Messiah? Did he run to Mary's house that night to tell her about his dream, or did he wait until the next morning? Was he excited or reserved? Who knows exactly what he felt, but one thing we know for certain, Joseph took Mary as his wife.

I am not sure Joseph really understood all that he had been told, nor all that would take place. No parents truly understand what they are getting into when they have a child. But this must be especially compounded when we consider that for Joseph and Mary their firstborn child is the Holy Son of God!

I am sure Joseph had questions, concerns, doubts, and fears. But Joseph trusts what the Lord had said, and in faith stepped out and lived it. That, I believe, is what Christmas through the eyes of Joseph would look like. It is walking by faith, even when we can't understand, are confused, or are afraid.

So often we equate having faith as having no doubt and fear. So often I have heard preachers explain having faith as not being afraid or leaving our questions behind. Allow me to be blunt: I do not accept this understanding of faith. Period.

Mary was faithful, but when the shepherds came to see the newborn king and told her and Joseph of all the angels said to them, the scripture records that *Mary treasured all these words and pondered them in her heart.*[39] "Pondered" means questioned, considered carefully, thought about. Having questions does not negate faith.

Nor does fear. I think back to the gospel of Mark and the account of Jesus praying in the Garden of Gethsemane. Mark records that Jesus is "distressed and agitated."[40] Jesus even tells Peter, James, and John that he is *deeply grieved, even to death*.[41] It is there in the garden that Jesus prays to the Father, *let this cup pass from me*.[42] I believe it is a safe assumption to say that Jesus was afraid and fearful. Yet we do not believe at any point Jesus lost faith, do we?

The author of the Letter to the Hebrews gives the following definition of faith: *Now faith is the assurance of things hoped for, the conviction of things not seen*.[43] Nowhere does the author of Hebrews claim that faith is not having doubt, fear, questions, concerns, or confusion. Rather, faith is having an assurance in something that is hoped for, and conviction, a strong belief and confession, of something that cannot yet be seen.

We see this understanding of faith as we dare to view Christmas through the eyes of Joseph. He is hoping in the promise of the Messiah, and undoubtedly gains a conviction to that end, even though he presumably does not live to witness with Mary the agony of their earthly Son's mission, nor the glory of the resurrection of Jesus as the Christ. So, I believe it is safe to say Joseph had a "conviction of things not seen."[44]

When we consider Joseph and what Christmas might have looked like through his eyes, we see

Christmas as a living out of the faith we profess. No matter the cost, or how little we understand, or what questions we might have, faith claims assurance in a hope given to us in the promise of God, and a conviction of something that our eyes have not yet seen.

Faith is the action of living our lives in this assurance and conviction. This we see through the eyes of Joseph as he responds at the invitation to the first Christmas. How will you respond to the invitation of this Christmas? What does Christmas look like through your eyes?

Thoughts From Chapter 3

How does wrestling with this perspective of Joseph challenge or change the ways you previously have thought about this passage? What new insights did you gain?

What Joseph hears from Mary is something that more than likely did not fit with the ways Joseph always understood God andGod's workings. In what ways are you not open to Gods' "new ways?"Are their blinders that you have to what God may be doing in your midst that is unexpected?

What does "having faith" mean to you? How did this perspective of Joseph challenge or grow your understanding of faith? Are you truly living by faith?

Did you see that!

Seeing Christmas as a Shepherd.

The Gospel of Luke 2:8-20[45]

In that region there were shepherds living in the fields, keeping watch over their flock by night. Then an angel of the Lord stood before them, and the glory of the Lord shone around them, and they were terrified. But the angel said to them, "Do not be afraid; for see—I am bringing you good news of great joy for all the people: to you is born this day in the city of David a Savior, who is the Messiah, the Lord. This will be a sign for you: you will find a child wrapped in bands of cloth and lying in a manger." And suddenly there was with the angel a multitude of the heavenly host, praising God and saying,

"Glory to God in the highest heaven, and on earth peace among those whom he favors!"

When the angels had left them and gone into heaven, the shepherds said to one another, "Let us go now to Bethlehem and see this thing that has taken place, which the Lord has made known to us." So they went with haste and found Mary and Joseph, and the child lying in the manger. When they saw this, they made known what had been told them about this child; and all who heard it were amazed at what the shepherds told them. But Mary treasured all these words and pondered them in her heart. The shepherds returned, glorifying and praising God for all they had heard and seen, as it had been told them.

Chapter 4
Christmas Through the Eyes of Shepherds

FOR MANY OF US, reading this part of the Christmas story brings to mind a whirlwind of nostalgic memories. We can slip into a sentimental stupor of sorts as we reminisce about Christmases of long ago. Possibly we recall children's programs where we, or our child, played the role of the angel delivering this message in their own sweet way. Maybe, like me, you found yourself as one of the shepherds, who always seemed to get into trouble. Perhaps we remember gathering with our church families on Christmas Eve and hearing this passage proclaimed. We might recollect gathering with our family on Christmas morning as the story of the angelic announcement to the Shepherds was read from the family Bible.

How ever we remember it, for us this passage brings excitement, hope, and awe. We get a flood of warm-fuzzy feelings and wistful images in our minds. But this was not the case for the first readers of Luke's gospel. This account was shocking, unheard of, and alarming. The fact that this passage is set in an open field, and the first to hear are a group of shepherds, would have been startling to those who first read it, to say the least. It would be shocking because God had chosen to proclaim this great, hopeful, and peaceful message in a sparsely populated countryside, in a violence-prone region, to a bunch of ragamuffin shepherds!

We have to understand that countrysides, roads, and small villages were havens for vagabonds, muggers, and criminals during this time. Consider the story of the rape of Dinah in Genesis 34, or the Parable of the Good Samaritan in Luke 10 as examples of the danger of countrysides and open roads. In our own day and time traveling in such places can still pose dangers. Dark alleyways, vacant parking garages, and empty buildings are some of our places that can cause anxiety and fear. But add to this the perception of shepherds in first-century Palestine, and you have one shocking setting and characters for such a divine announcement. It would have been as startling for them to hear of shepherds receiving such a message as it would be for us to imagine an angel visiting Congress and giving such an address!

It may not be easy for us to accept that shepherds weren't held in high regard. This can be confusing because of how the image of the shepherd is treated in scripture. However, we need to understand that the image was one thing, while the reality of shepherds was another.

Shepherds in that day were often involved in conflict with other people over land boundaries. They had a tendency for violence.[46] Shepherds would intentionally allow their sheep to graze in someone else's fields. In fact, on a rabbinical list of occupations, "good Jews" would not allow their children to grow up to be shepherds. This was because it was impossible for shepherds to keep all of the ritual laws.[47]

With all this in mind, imagine how shocking it was for Luke's readers to hear that an angel of God Almighty would come to a bunch of shepherds in a remote countryside and declare "Peace!" But what is really amazing is that these shepherds would leave their flocks in the middle of the night to travel a fair distance to a village called Bethlehem just to witness what the angel had proclaimed.

Far from the cute, quiet little Christmas story we have all imagined this to be lies the heart of the angelic message. The *good news to all people*[48] has the power to lift up the lowly, the dispossessed, the rejected, and the violent. The message of God that declares the grace of God has come to *everyone*!

What better setting to declare peace than in a scene that is known for violence? Who better to first receive this message than a group of people who were despised? What better location to declare a communal miracle than in a place that was lonely? This angelic sermon, set in this countryside, and given to shepherds, in a lonely field, proclaims to us that the way things are is not the way they were intended to be. This message declares to the entire world that God knows what is happening, and God has come to do something about it!

Here in this passage we see shepherds — rough, tough, dirty, stinky, rejected, refused, feared shepherds coming to a new light. This light, as first seen by them in the angelic host as, *the glory of the Lord shown all around them,*[49] called them into a new understanding, a new relationship, as the light of the Christ shines brilliantly to dispel the darkness of night. The shepherds take on a more glorious image as they come to the light and seek out the one who has come to be the "Good Shepherd."[50] Jesus, the Savior of the World, has come to truly be our Good Shepherd. He has come to save, protect, and guide the entire fold of God.

The angelic proclamation to such a group in such a place challenges our perceptions of what God can do, who God is, and what God seeks to accomplish. We are forced to rethink where God will choose to appear, and whom God will accept. This is further experienced in the life and ministry of Jesus.

Jesus eats with sinners and heals the sick. He calls tax collectors, fishermen, and other ordinary "sinners" to follow him. Here we get a foreshadowing of what the Christ has come to do, and to whom the Christ has come.

The shepherds left their flocks, abandoned what they thought they knew, to seek something new that God was giving unto them. We also are called and challenged to leave what we think we know, and seek out what new life God is bringing to us and to the world. We are invited to open ourselves to the new creation God is bringing, even in unexpected, and perhaps unperceived, ways.

I believe that if we could see Christmas through the eyes of the shepherds we would see it as being about second chances. Christmas through their eyes gives to us a vision of the forgiving grace and the work of reclaiming a fallen creation that God has come in Christ Jesus to do. It does not matter that the countryside where we are currently found is a place of violence, for it will be a place of peace. Just as wolves lying down with lambs may not be the current reality, it will be.[51]

These shepherds became more than mere herders when they journeyed to Bethlehem. They became the first witnesses to the light of the world breaking through the darkness of sin. You see, Christmas is not about the way things are. Rather Christmas is about the way things can be, are supposed to be, and are promised to be. God has come to restore all of creation. Isaac Watts, the author of the words to one of my favorite carols, "Joy to the World," declares this beautifully in the third stanza: *No more let sins and sorrows grow, nor thorns infest the ground. He comes to make his blessings flow far as the curse is found.*[52]

Christmas declares to us that even the way we are right now is not the way we can be, are suppose to be, and are promised to be. We are, as the apostle Paul writes, "a new creation."[53] The Christ has come to free us from all that hinders and binds us. Again looking at Paul, we see him write to the Church at Rome, *Do not be conformed to this world, but be transformed by the renewing of your minds, so that you may discern what is the will of God—what is good and acceptable and perfect.*[54]

We are no longer chained to the desires and will of the world as it is currently. In fact, we are called to join God in the mammoth task of changing the world! The birth of the Christ that the shepherds dare to proclaim is a powerful, earth-shattering demonstration of the extravagance of God's grace!

This angelic pronouncement to which the shepherds testify leaves nothing out. There is no room left for questions concerning what God is doing. It is a blunt message sent from Almighty God telling the world what is happening. There is glory and peace that comes from God, who is in the highest heaven, to all the people of the world. In fact, God is *with* us! *To you is born this day in the city of David a Savior.*[55] It is personal. This glorious promise being fulfilled is not given in a generalized manner. Rather, it is given to the world, to shepherds, to me, and to you, <u>personally</u>.

This day a Savior is given *to you*. It is a message that should make us stop and awaken from our mundane routines and judgmental views about the world and the people who live in it. We, like the shepherds, should be shocked and amazed, and even a little fearful, at the awesomeness and abundance of God's grace being poured out. Seeing Christmas from the perspective of the shepherds cries out to us that no matter where we have come from, despite where we find ourselves, regardless of what we have done, for all the struggles we have faced or failures we have experienced, Emmanuel, *God is with us,*[56] has arrived!

Further, the Promised One of God is not locked away in some luxurious palace, far removed from the issues of this life and this world as it is right now. No, the Christ is born in humility, accessibility, and gentleness. He can be found not clothed in the finest of linens, but in simple bands of cloth. Royal bodyguards, who would be quick to banish any who might come, do not guard him. Rather, the Christ can be found lying in a manger where even the animals may gaze upon him.

He did not come as a conqueror who would strike fear into the hearts of those who would oppose him. Rather, Jesus the Christ, Almighty God, was birthed as a human child. He was born like *us*, grew like *us*, and experienced life like *us*. He then died *for us,* and on the third day rose again for *us* to conquer sin, death, and hell for all time, *for us!*

Christmas through the eyes of the shepherds shows us we have a God of second chances. God has come to bring love, hope, joy, and peace to people who will seek it, and in places where it is not currently found. Through the eyes of the shepherds we see that you, I, everyone, in fact, the entire world can all receive another chance.

The way things might be right now is not the way they have to be or will remain. Relationships that are broken can be mended. Hurts are capable of being comforted. Anger is able to be relieved. We can learn how to offer forgiveness, as well as grasp its reception. In short, God's grace abounds!

Hear this angelic proclamation anew, and see the glory of God with shepherd's eyes. Allow it to speak powerfully shocking to your life, and may it be emblazed upon your heart. *Do not be afraid; for see—I am bringing* <u>you</u> *good news of great joy for all the people: to you is born this day in the city of David a Savior, who is the Messiah, the Lord.*[57]

What response will we give to this invitation to go and see? Will we stay in the countryside and the flocks of that which we think we know? Perhaps we will dare journey to a little village and accept the offer of a second chance. There we will find the

Messiah waiting for us as a child in a manger, to become our King of Kings and Lord of Lords, our Savior and Redeemer. There will be no rejection, no broken promises, and no recalling of our past failures. There will be only love.

When we see the first Christmas through the eyes of the shepherds we behold grace abounding! When we, with the shepherds, keep watch and witness the angelic visitation, we too receive the proclamation of great joy. We are offered nothing less than second chances. Will you dare to claim them? If not, what will you claim this Christmas? How will this Christmas proclamation to a bunch of shepherds be perceived through your eyes?

Thoughts from Chapter 4

What "warm-fuzzy" understandings of the Christmas Story does this perspective challenge for you?

Have you ever considered Christmas as being about a second chance? How does this claim challenge or grow your understanding of the meaning of Christmas?

Where in your life do you need a second, third, or fourth chance? Can you believe and accept that God wants to give you such in a new life? How can this Christmas be a second chance for you?

What WAS God thinking?

Seeing Christmas though the eyes of God.

The Gospel of Luke 2:1-7

*In those days a decree went out from Emperor
Augustus that all the world should be registered. This was the
first registration and was taken while Quirinius was governor
of Syria. All went to their own towns to be registered. Joseph
also went from the town of Nazareth in Galilee to Judea, to
the city of David called Bethlehem, because he was descended
from the house and family of David. He went to be registered
with Mary, to whom he was engaged and who was expecting a
child. While they were there, the time came for her to deliver
her child. And she gave birth to her firstborn son and
wrapped him in bands of cloth, and laid him in a manger,
because there was no room for them in the inn.*[58]

The Gospel of John 1:1-5,14-18

*In the beginning was the Word, and the Word was with
God, and the Word was God. He was in the beginning with
God. All things came into being through him, and without
him not one thing came into being. What has come into being
in him was life, and the life was the light of all people. The
light shines in the darkness, and the darkness did not
overcome it...And the Word became flesh and lived among us,
and we have seen his glory, the glory as of a father's only son,
full of grace and truth. (John testified to him and cried out,
"This is he of whom I said, 'He who comes after me ranks
ahead of me because he was before me.'") From his fullness
we have received, grace upon grace. The law indeed was given
through Moses; grace and truth came through Jesus Christ.
No one has ever seen God. It is God the only Son, who is
close to the Father's heart, who has made him known.*[59]

Chapter 5

Christmas Through the Eyes of God

THROUGH THE PAST chapters we have sought to explore and envision what the first Christmas might have looked like through the eyes of those who were there to experience it. We have considered the different perspectives each narrative brings. We have wrestled with notions each story reveals. Let us review for a moment where we have journeyed.

In considering John the Baptizer we proposed that perhaps Christmas through his eyes would be about preparation. This preparation for which John is proclaiming is not about cooking, shopping, or traveling. Rather it is about preparing our hearts and lives to receive the Advent, the coming, of the Christ. We prepare to celebrate and remember the First Advent, when the Christ came as the Child of

Bethlehem. But the call is also to prepare for the Second Advent, when the Christ will return as the King of Kings and Lord of Lords.

When we considered Mary, we proposed Christmas through her eyes might be about self-sacrifice. Mary willingly responded to the call of God. Her response to Gabriel was, *Here am I, the servant of the Lord; let it be with me according to your word.*[60] With that, Mary presented herself to the blessing of God for a life of joy, pain, and amazement. Her self-sacrificing life causes us to rethink what it means to be blessed by God.

Next we considered what Joseph might have experienced and considered Christmas to be by attempting to view it though his eyes. We wrestled with the notion that Christmas might look like stepping out in faith. We see through Joseph that faith is not about always understanding, or not having questions. On the contrary, faith is being willing to walk on the journey as God calls, even when the way is not fully known.

In the previous chapter we saw the shepherds keeping lonely vigil over their flock in the countryside when they heard the angelic proclamation. We saw how shocking the setting and first recipients of this message would have been to the first readers of Luke's gospel. This led us to suppose that Christmas through their eyes might be about second chances. The proclamation of "Peace" is to everyone, in all the world, and in all times and places. The way things are currently is not the way they are intended to be. The way things are now is not how it will remain. All creation is being renewed as the light of the Christ breaks through the darkness.

But none of these people, as important as they are to understanding the story of Christmas, are really the center or focus of the narrative. They are a part of the story, but they did not write it. They receive the gift of Christmas, but they are not the ones who gave it. The main character in the Christmas drama that is proclaimed in the Holy Word is none other than God. This brings us to our question: "What might Christmas look like through God's eyes?"

This is a huge undertaking! After all, I do not claim to be able to know or understand the mind of God. Who can fully understand God? After all, God speaks through the prophet Isaiah: *For my thoughts are not your thoughts, nor are my ways your ways, says the LORD.*[61] But with all such things considered, I do not think we are being disrespectful or arrogant to seek to ponder what Christmas might mean to the one who gave it. After all, it is God that so often gets pushed aside in our modern celebrations and traditions of the holiday. Maybe daring to take some time to consider Christmas from the heavenly perspective could help us reclaim the truth in our lives.

First, let us look at the two passages we are reading to gain some perspective about this question. The first, from the gospel of Luke, tells us quite simply about the actual birth of Jesus the Christ. The Roman world had been ordered to pay taxes, so a census or registration was needed. Each family was to journey to the hometown of the head of the household in order to register. We must remember, in this day and time the husband was considered legally the head of the household. So, since Joseph was from Bethlehem, he journeyed back there from Nazareth, with Mary, in order to pay his taxes.

Then it happened. While they were there Mary gave birth, and the Promised One of God came into the world. Such an unexpected way for God to enter the world, don't you think? But of course, when we consider the other parts that compose this story, we see nothing about it is expected!

Mary was going about her regular routine when Gabriel showed up to tell her "Congratulations! You are highly favored by God!"[62] Joseph was taken aback when he first heard the news and stayed up half the night trying to figure out what to do. Finally, when he did fall asleep, an angel of the Lord appeared to tell him what Mary had said was true, and he should not be afraid to take her as his wife.[63] Furthermore, who would have invited shepherds to come see a baby that was newly born? Shepherds could not get in unannounced to see the king, but undoubtedly anyone is welcome to come barging in on Almighty God![64] And while we are at it, who really expected God to come as a baby in the first place? To be wrapped in bands of cloth? To be found lying in a manger? None of this is what is expected.

So, of course, Jesus would be born when they are away from home, after a long and tiring journey, and registering to pay taxes. I can't help wondering if when they were preparing to leave, Joseph ever looked at Mary, or vise-versa, and said, "Gee, I hope this baby doesn't decide to come while we're in Bethlehem!"

I know that when my wife and I were expecting our first child, I was so incredibly nervous. During this time we were preparing to move to a new appointment. Of course, the moving day was not far from our child's due date. Suffice it to say, we had some trepidation! I am sure it was nothing compared to what Mary and Joseph might have been feeling, but it was enough to make me appreciate this passage a little more.

When we consider the whole Christmas story with all of its implications, of course Jesus would be born in Bethlehem! What better way for the Promised Messiah to spin worldly understanding on its head than to come on a mandated journey, to pay taxes to oppressive pagans, and have the likes of shepherds show up to welcome his birth. It was totally unexpected and out of place. But that's what makes it all about God.

In my way of thinking, the unexpected and out of place are hallmarks of God. God always seems to show up when we least expect it, and in the most unlikely of circumstances. I have been amazed in my life to find God in places I would never have thought to look. Who expects to find God in places like bars, school buses, jail cells, and even a fraternity house? Who knew that when the scriptures talk about Christ coming to the "least to these" it was being literal.

It seems that Christmas though the eyes of God might look like taking the world by glorious surprise. Christmas from God's perspective, I believe, is about declaring grace unconditionally and unmerited upon everyone. That definitely squares with the angelic proclamation to the shepherds about "good news to all people."[65]

Someone told me years ago when I was confessing that I was surprised God would call me to the pastoral ministry, "Well, that's the problem with a Living God. A Living God can sure surprise the heck out of you!" Christmas is God's great "Surprise!" Christmas is God's ultimate revelation. Here God is, as one of us, to be with us, to reconcile us back to God's self. It is something for which we prepare. We know of Jesus' First Coming as a child among us. And we know of Christ's Second Coming, though we know not the time. But we must recognize that we live betwixt these two Advents.

One proclaims something past; the other, something future. What about the present?

The present is how we live each day. We are called to prepare <u>now</u> for life lived complete in the eternal presence of God. We seek each day to become more and more like our Creator, and subsequently, less and less like the world.

The present calls us to be self-sacrificing, as Jesus showed us in his own life, death, and resurrection. It will require us to walk by faith, even when we are unsure or do not fully understand. Above all, it gives us another chance—no matter where we have been or what we have done. The big "surprise" is that it is happening again, right now, this and every Christmas. And please make no mistake, the coming of the Christ and the blessings of the Kingdom of God are not only during the Christmas season. Everyday Christ is being born anew in our hearts and lives.

Even in the most unlikely places where we least expect it, God has a way of appearing. God interrupts our plans, causes us to rethink what we consider important, invites us to seemingly impossible tasks, and empowers us to do nothing less than change the world. That is why I believe Christmas through the eyes of God would look like the greatest, most glorious surprise in all of history.

Here comes God barging in, arriving in the most unexpected ways, and in the least expected places to declare that an unanticipated new creation is beginning right now in our midst. But upon what can we base this idea? Where do we get this notion? Consider with me the second passage we have read. It is from the gospel of John.

When Matthew and Luke talk about the beginning, they talk about Jesus' birth. However, when John talks about the beginning, he goes back to THE BEGINNING! If you will notice, the opening verses of John's gospel remind us of the opening verses of Genesis.

In these verses the author of the Gospel of John proclaims some deeply profound understandings. First, the birth of the Christ is not separate from God. Rather, the Christ *is* God. God has come to us as fully human, yet still being fully divine. Second, Jesus is the Word that was spoken that created all things. He is, from the beginning, *with* God *and* God. Third, the Word that is God dared to put on flesh like us, be born like us, and live as one of us. We come to know God not from philosophical rhetoric, but because we have seen God though Jesus.

We have seen the glory of God because we have witnessed the glory of the Christ. Finally, we know grace and truth through our Savior and Lord. To use the traditional Trinitarian language of the Church: because we know the Son, we know the Father. Because of the coming of Jesus, we have received both grace and truth.

But why? Why would the Father send the Son in the first place? John 3:16 tells us. *For God so loved the world that he gave his only Son, so that everyone who believes in him may not perish, but have eternal life.*[66] It is for love. This love is pure, self-sacrificing love. This is the second part of the way Christmas might appear through the eyes of God. If the statement begins "Surprise!" then it concludes, "I love you."

Many of us have heard before that God loves us. In fact, many of us wrestle with the depth of love God has for us. Some cannot fathom that God could possibly love them. For all of us who have, or will ever, wrestle with understanding and accepting God's love for us I say, "Behold Christmas." For those who have no problem accepting that God loves them, and who maybe just accept it without much thought I say, "Behold Christmas."

When we see the love of God as declared at Christmas, I hope it overwhelms our understandings and startles our senses. I pray when we experience God's love at Christmas we grab it with our hearts and refuse to let go until we know it more. When we attempt to see Christmas through the eyes of God it should cause us to rethink what we claim to understand about God. Seeing Christmas through God's eyes compels us to be open to the varied ways God unexpectedly appears and is at work in our lives and in the world. Christmas through God's eyes challenges us to behold the great love God has for us, for all people, and for all of Creation.

Through the eyes of God you and I become a part of the Christmas story. The entire world is invited to join in the chorus the angels sing proclaiming, *"Glory to God in the highest heaven, and on earth peace among those whom he favors!"*[67] Christmas through the eyes of God says nothing less than, "Surprise! God loves you."

So, prepare to be taken by surprise as God appears in unexpected ways and places. Understand that we are called to live this life in self-sacrifice to others, as God has shown self-sacrifice to us. Be ready and have courage to journey in the faith we profess. Be willing to embrace the truth that you have another chance, another life, through God's grace. And, above all, be opened to the great love God has for you.

I believe this is what Christmas looks like through the eyes of God. Are you able to see this as Christmas through yours?

Thoughts from Chapter 5

How has God unexpectedly appeared in your life? Where has God "surprised" you?

What changes in our understanding when we see Christmas as being about the surprise of God's love for us?

What are you going to do with all this now?

What Gifts?

Perceiving Christmas through Magi's eyes.

The Gospel of Matthew 2:1-12

In the time of King Herod, after Jesus was born in Bethlehem of Judea, wise men from the East came to Jerusalem, asking, "Where is the child who has been born king of the Jews? For we observed his star at its rising, and have come to pay him homage." When King Herod heard this, he was frightened, and all Jerusalem with him; and calling together all the chief priests and scribes of the people, he inquired of them where the Messiah was to be born. They told him, "In Bethlehem of Judea; for so it has been written by the prophet:

'And you, Bethlehem, in the land of Judah,
are by no means least among the rulers of Judah;
for from you shall come a ruler
who is to shepherd my people Israel.'"

Then Herod secretly called for the wise men and learned from them the exact time when the star had appeared. Then he sent them to Bethlehem, saying, "Go and search diligently for the child; and when you have found him, bring me word so that I may also go and pay him homage." When they had heard the king, they set out; and there, ahead of them, went the star that they had seen at its rising, until it stopped over the place where the child was. When they saw that the star had stopped, they were overwhelmed with joy. On entering the house, they saw the child with Mary his mother; and they knelt down and paid him homage. Then, opening their treasure-chests, they offered him gifts of gold, frankincense, and myrrh. And having been warned in a dream not to return to Herod, they left for their own country by another road.

Chapter 6
Christmas Through the Eyes of the Magi

IT MIGHT APPEAR ODD to discuss the Magi now. After all, it seems as though once we have considered Christmas through the eyes of God then the story would be complete. By contemplating Christmas through God's eyes we see the pronouncement of "Surprise! God loves you." But what is the extent of that love? Though God definitely has the final word, there is still one aspect of the Christmas narrative to be examined. The visit of the Magi fulfills the ultimate proclamation as to whom the Christ truly is, and what the Christ has come to do.

The Magi themselves are a mystery. So much of what we believe about them is based on myth and legend rather than actual scriptural scholarship. For instance, so often we assume there were three of them. But the scriptures do not mention how many Magi made the journey, only that three types of gifts were presented.[68] I have heard it stated that these Magi were from the Orient. After all, a popular Epiphany carol's opening stanza sings, "We three kings of Orient are."[69] However, when we search the scriptural text all we find stated is, ...*wise men from the East came to Jerusalem...*[70]

This raises the question, "Where from the East?" Is it the Far East, the greater Middle East, or simply east of Jerusalem?

This carol brings us to another claim; that these visitors were royal. But the verses that contain the account of the Magi never tell us they were kings. The only title ascribed to them in the Matthean gospel are "magi." In fact, we do not know who they were. The Bible never even mentions their names. There are many scholars who have researched these particular questions, and others like them, seeking to find some answer to the quandaries that surround these learned travelers who have come from the east in order to pay homage to the child Messiah.

As a point, with the amount of basic information that is lacking, it might seem impossible to ponder how Christmas through the eyes of the Magi might have appeared. But I believe it is no accidental forfeiture due to the rolling of the ages that this information is lost. Rather, it is my persuasion that such facts about the Magi themselves are purposely negated in order to force us to render from the text that which the author of the gospel of Matthew truly desires us to witness. But what is this witness? The answer can be found in the journey and the gifts themselves, not in the persons who dared to travel far or brought them. By considering the journey and the gifts, we can propose how Christmas for the Magi possibly appeared.

Let us consider what we can know from the text. We know these Magi are at least astrologers, for they have followed a star. They saw a star rise that was uncommon in the night sky, and discerned that it heralded a proclamation of the birth of the True King. How can we say the Magi saw the Christ as "the True King?" Because these Magi were not from Jerusalem, Judea, or the Roman Empire. This is the reason they had audience with King Herod; to gain permission to travel through his land. They must have been of some importance since Herod himself met with them. But also Herod may have met with them because of the message they had brought. They came telling that they were journeying through his land to pay homage to the child who had been born King of the Jews. This was upsetting to Herod, as no new heir to his throne had been born in his own household.

These Magi, from some kingdom or kingdoms not of Judea or Rome, who apparently were not themselves Jewish, had come to bow before a child they held as greater than themselves, the rulers they represented, or their own religious views. They had traveled following a star. They had come bearing gifts. They came to worship the Promised One of God. This journeying of Magi in and of itself tells us that the Messiah that has been born was not going to be for Israel alone. This Messiah has come for the world.

As powerful as considering the journey can be, there are also the gifts to explore. The gifts that we are told the Magi brought are gold, frankincense, and myrrh.[71] If you think about it for a moment, the gifts the Magi offered are strange to give a child. Who gives gold to a child? A savings bond perhaps, but it would be unusual to present gold coins to a baby or toddler. When you ponder frankincense and myrrh it becomes even more confusing.

As bizarre as it may be, these gifts are considered literal gifts. I truly believe these are the offerings the Magi gave. However, there are more to the gifts than the sum of their parts. They are also symbolic. The gifts point beyond themselves in powerful ways.

The first gift offered was gold. In antiquity gold was often used as a presentation of tribute. The Old Testament is filled with references to the presentation of gold as an offering, gift, and adornment.[72] We can learn from historical studies that gold was given in presentation to kings and rulers.

When we ponder the fact that the Magi have traveled to pay homage to the child that has been born King of the Jews, then we begin to understand why they would have offered Jesus gold. They have brought Jesus gold because he is the King. This is foreshadowing what we will learn later on as we continue reading in the Gospel of Matthew—Jesus is the King of Kings.

The next gift to consider is that of frankincense. Frankincense was a key ingredient used in making the incense for the Sanctuary of the Temple.[73] In fact, many believe it was used throughout the Ancient Near East as a perfume for the worship of a deity. When we reflect on this gift, and that the Magi had come and knelt before the child Jesus, we can see another act of symbolic prophecy emerge. Th e Magi recognized the Christ as God.

This is a foundational understanding as to whom we consider Jesus to be. We do not simply believe Jesus is a messenger of God, but that Jesus *is* God. The Incarnation proclaims that Jesus is God made fl esh. Here, by the Magi, we already see this proclamation being made.

The fi nal gift we are told the Magi brought was myrrh. Of all of the gifts presented, this is the most peculiar. In antiquity myrrh had many uses, but one of the most common was to embalm bodies.[74] How would you feel if someone gave your child embalming fluid as a gift?

Yet here we see the Magi offer to the Christ not only gold and frankincense, but also myrrh. These Magi, truly wise as they were, recognized that Jesus was going to die. Th is may not be something that is, of itself, a mystery. We all understand that mortal life ends in death. But, when we view what we have already learned about the Magi, we know there is more to this than uninvolved biology. They are prophesying in this gift the sacrifice of Jesus on the cross for us. The Christ has been born to die.

So often when we celebrate Christmas we only observe the birth. We proclaim the message of the angels, we journey with the shepherds, and we marvel at the manger. But just as Christmas is about the birth of the Christ, it is also marking his death.

Without Christmas there would be no cross; yet without the cross there would be no power in Christmas. We must not forget here at the end what we struggled with in the first chapter with the proclamation of John the Baptizer. John's proclamation is about preparing for the coming of the Christ. We prepare not only for the First Advent of our Lord as the Child of Bethlehem, but also look for his Second Advent when he returns as the King of Kings. If we do not behold the Cross and Resurrection at the same time that we behold the Manger and the Star, then we have not prepared for the full message of Christmas.

We cannot neglect what we have learned by imagining Christmas through Mary's eyes. We must be willing to be called and used according to God's will. This is without hesitation, no matter the cost. We saw how Mary was "blessed." We heard Simeon foretell Mary that *a sword will pierce your own soul too.*[75] By seeing Christmas from the Magi's perspective we cannot ignore that behind the glorious message the season brings lies the call of following.

In wrestling along with Joseph as he learned that his betrothed was with child from God, we discovered that Christmas from his perspective is about walking by faith, even when we do not fully understand. We saw that God can do amazing, new things. God can act in ways we might have never before considered. When we couple this with the viewpoint we gain from the Magi we see that God, from the first Christmas, was setting out to do something new and unexpected. We have a God who is our King, and who is willing to lay down his life for us. Who would have ever thought this would be?

As we beheld the angelic proclamation with the shepherds we were made aware that, no matter what we had done, we could receive a second chance. We found that we can come to God just as we are and enter into God's divine presence. Christmas with the Magi's understanding proclaims to us the greatness and the cost of that second chance we are given. We go forth proclaiming to all the world what we have seen and experienced because we discover the great love and grace that makes that second chance possible.

By considering how Christmas might be seen through the eyes of the Magi we are forced to leave all of the trimmings and trappings of the season, and enter into the fullness of the One who has been born among us. The fullness of perceiving Christmas through the eyes of God comes into complete focus in the journey and gifts of the Magi. "Surprise! God loves you"—so much so that God has come in Christ Jesus to be not only our King and God, but also our Sacrifice.

The gift of Christmas is nothing less than salvation. The forgiveness of sins, the "good news of great joy," the second chances this Christmas affords comes as a gift to us, but at great cost to God. This is the fullness of the passage from the Gospel of John that we have reflected upon so often through this journey: *For God so loved the world that he gave his only Son, so that everyone who believes in him may not perish but may have eternal life. Indeed, God did not send the Son into the world to condemn the world, but in order that the world might be saved through him.*[76]

I may reject the interpretations of the carol "We Three Kings" as it references royalty or location of the Magi, but I can unequivocally say that it powerfully and truthfully proclaims all that the Magi foretell about Jesus the Christ in its second through fifth stanzas:

Born a King on Bethlehem's plain; gold I bring to crown him again, King forever, ceasing never, over us all to reign.

Frankincense to offer have I; incense owns a Deity nigh; prayer and praising, voices raising, worshipping God on high.

Myrrh is mine; its bitter perfume breathes a life of gathering gloom; sorrowing, sighing, bleeding, dying, sealed in a stone-cold tomb.

Glorious now behold him arise; King, and God, and Sacrifice: Alleluia, Alleluia, sounds through the earth and skies.[77]

Now we come to the end of this Christmas journey. However, we find that the journey continues. By seeing Christmas through the eyes of the Magi, we find in the Child of the Manger that which we might already know, but yet somehow gets forgotten in the ways we live in this season. We have the King of Kings, Almighty God, and the Lamb of God, who takes away the sin of the world. Let us hear the full message Christmas proclaims. Let us celebrate Christmas in the fullness of this message. May we be found as wise as the Magi, willing to follow the Bright Morning Star, and living each day paying homage to our King, our God, and our Sacrifice.

This is how I imagine Christmas was seen by the Magi. How does this vision compare with yours?

Thoughts From Chapter 6

Have you considered the journey and gifts of the Magi before in the symbolic messages they bring? How does this understanding expand and/or challenge the ways you have previously thought about the narrative of the Magi?

How does reflecting on the cross during Christmas present a challenge or discomfort for you? How do you see it as completing the Christmas story?

The Magi brought gifts of gold, frankincense, and myrrh to pay homage to the Christ based in their understanding and belief as to who Jesus is. What gift(s) would you bring to the Christ, and why?

In considering all that we have journeyed with throughout this study, how has your celebration of Christmas been challenged and/or changed?

Conclusion

We have journeyed through the Christmas story pondering what Christmas might have looked like through the eyes of those who first experienced it. But the story of Christmas is far from over. As was stated, you and I are a part of the continuing story of God's grace and love that Christmas begins.

It is my hope and prayer that this journey has challenged you, maybe conflicted you, caused you to think, and brought you comfort and peace—all at the same time! That is what occurs on a journey. A journey has many twists and turns. The unexpected happens. There are different experiences to be had along the way. The journey of Christmas is an amazing narrative of God's grace and love for us, and for the entire world.

Our journey together through this particular reflection is now ending. What happens now? The final discussion question in Chapter 5 is really the most challenging for me. The question is, "What are we going to do with it?"

This was not meant as a theological exercise, or a collection of interesting thoughts. It is one thing to consider these perspectives; it is quite another to live them. May the blessings of Christmas, and the call it issues, be a part of our lives every day of the year. And now I say to you, in humility, joyfulness, and all sincerity: Merry Christmas!

Endnotes and References

1. *It"s the Most Wonderful Time of the Year* is a Christmas song written in 1963 by Edward Pola and George Wyle. Referenced from Wikipedia.
2. John 1:19-29. The Scripture quotations contained herein are from the New Revised Standard Version Bible, copyright 1989, by the Division of Christian Education of the National Council of the Churches of Christ in the U.S.A. Used by permission. All rights reserved.
3. John 3:16-17
4. Luke 1:5-25; 57-80
5. Luke 1:16-17
6. Luke 1:41
7. Luke 1:39-45
8. Matthew 3:1-4
9. See Matthew 3: 5-6 and Luke 3: 10-14
10. John 1:29
11. Matthew 23:25-28
12. Matthew 23:25
13. Matthew 23:27
14. Reference John 1:29; author's paraphrase.
15. Reference John 1:29; author's paraphrase with emphasis added.
16. Reference from Dr. Seuss, *How the Grinch Stole Christmas*, New York: Random House Publishers; 1957,1983.
17. Luke 1:10 author's paraphrase.
18. John 1:29
19. Luke 1:26-38
20. Rowell, Edward K. and Leadership Journal, *1001 Quotes, Illustrations, and Humorous Stories*, Grand Rapids: Baker Books, originally published as three books, "Quotes and Ideas Starters for Preachers and Teachers" (1996), "Fresh

Illustrations for Preaching and Teaching" (1997), and "Preaching and Teaching" (1996); 461.

21. See "The Great Commandment," Matthew 22: 36-40
22. Matthew 1:1-17
23. Author's paraphrase
24. James 1:17, author's paraphrase
25. Luke 2:22-35, verse 35 specific
26. Luke 9:23-25
27. Matthew 1:18-25
28. Matthew 1:1-17
29. Matthew 2:18-25 and Luke 2:1-21
30. Matthew 2:13-15, referenced
31. Luke 2:22-ff
32. Luke 2:41-ff
33. Edershem, Alfred. *Sketches of Jewish Social Life*, Peabody: Hendrickson Publishers, Inc., 1994; 137.
34. Matthew 1:19
35. Gardner, Paul D., ed., *New International Encyclopedia of Bible Characters*. Grand Rapids; 1995, 375.
36. www.thinkexist.com (Accessed May 30, 2012).
37. Psalm 51:10, referenced
38. Isaiah 7:14
39. Luke 2:19
40. Mark 14:33
41. Mark 14:34
42. Mark 14:32-36
43. Hebrews 11:1
44. Hebrews 11:1, referenced
45. Luke 2:8-20
46. see *The Works of Josephus*
47. Culpepper, Alan R., Leander E. Keck, Thomas G. Long, Bruce C. Birch, Katheryan Pfisterer Darr, James Earl Massey, Marion L. Soards, David L. Petersen, John J.

Collins, William L. Lane, Gail R. O'Day, Eds., *New Interpreters Bible Commentary, Volume IX*. Nashville; Abingdon Press; 1995, 65.

48. Luke 2:10, referenced

49. Luke 2:9

50. John 10:11-ff, referenced

51. Isaiah 11:6, referenced

52. Watts, Isaac, lyrics, 1719 (based on Psalm 98: 4-9) music arranged from G.F. Handel 1741 by Lowell Mason, 1848., "Joy to the World," as found in *The United Methodist Hymnal*; Nashville: The United Methodist Publishing House; 1989, 246.

53. 2 Corinthians 5:17, referenced

54. Romans 12:2

55. Luke 2:11, referenced

56. God is with us is the meaning of the name "Emmanuel." See Matthew 1:23

57. Luke 2:10-11, emphasis added

58. Luke 2:1-7

59. John 1:1-5, 14-18

60. Luke 1:38

61. Isaiah 55:8

62. Luke 1:28, paraphrase reference

63. Author's interpretation and paraphrase reference to Matthew 1:18-25

64. Author's interpretation and paraphrase reference of Luke 2:8-20

65. Luke 2:10, reference

66. John 3:16

67. Luke 2:14

68. Matthew 2:11

69. Hopkins, John H., Jr., music and lyrics, 1857, "We Three Kings" as found in *The United Methodist Hymnal*; Nashville: The United Methodist Publishing House; 1989, 254.

70. Matthew 2:1

71. Matthew 2:11

72. See Genesis 24:22-53, 41:42; also Exodus 25:23-30, 26:5-6 as examples.

73. Brand, Chad, Charles Draper, and Archie England, General Editors; Holman Illustrated Bible Dictionary, Nashville: Holman Reference, Holman Bible Publishers; 2003, 600.

74. Brand, Chad, Charles Draper, and Archie England, General Editors; Holman Illustrated Bible Dictionary, Nashville: Holman Reference, Holman Bible Publishers; 2003, 1163.

75. Luke 2:35

76. John 3:16-17

77. Hopkins, John H., Jr., music and lyrics, 1857, "We Three Kings" as found in *The United Methodist Hymnal*; Nashville: The United Methodist Publishing House; 1989, 254.

Made in United States
Troutdale, OR
11/06/2024

24506481R00066